Your Free Gift

As a special Thank You for downloading this book I have put together an exclusive report on Morning Habits.

MORNING HABITS
HOW TO BUILD A MORNING ROUTINE

Includes Sample Morning Routines And Tips To Creating Your Own

Learn how to build your own morning routine to achieve increased productivity and less stress. Includes sample morning routines and exclusive tips towards creating your own.

>> You Can Download This Free Report By Clicking Here <<

TABLE OF CONTENTS

Introduction

Chapter 1

Chapter 2

Chapter 3

Chapter 4

Chapter 5

Chapter 6

Chapter 7

Chapter 8

Chapter 9

Chapter 10

Chapter 11

Chapter 12

Chapter 13

Chapter 14

Chapter 15

Chapter 16

Chapter 17

Chapter 18

Chapter 19

Chapter 20

MOTHER TERESA

40 INSPIRATIONAL LIFE LESSONS AND TIMELESS WISDOM FROM THE LIFE OF MOTHER TERESA

Scarlett Johnson

COPYRIGHT

Copyright © 2015

All rights reserved. This book or any portion thereof may not be reproduced or used in any manner whatsoever without the express written permission of the publisher except for the use of brief quotations in a book review or scholarly journal.

Disclaimer

All rights reserved. No part of this publication may be reproduced, distributed, or transmitted in any form or by any means, including photocopying, recording, or other electronic or mechanical methods, without the prior written permission of the publisher, except in the case of brief quotations embodied in critical reviews and certain other noncommercial uses permitted by copyright law.

Kindle 5 Star Books

Free Kindle 5 Star Book Club Membership

Join Other Kindle 5 Star Members Who Are Getting Private Access To Weekly Free Kindle Book Promotions

Get free Kindle books

Stay connected:

Join our Facebook group

Follow Kindle 5 Star on Twitter

Also, if you want to receive updates on Entrepreneur Publishing's new books, free promotions and Kindle countdown deals sign up to their New Release Mailing List.

For entrepreneurs: http://www.entrepreneurfinesse.com

CHAPTER 21

CHAPTER 22

CHAPTER 23

CHAPTER 24

CHAPTER 25

CHAPTER 26

CHAPTER 27

CHAPTER 28

CHAPTER 29

CHAPTER 30

CHAPTER 31

CHAPTER 32

CHAPTER 33

CHAPTER 34

CHAPTER 35

CHAPTER 36

CHAPTER 37

CHAPTER 38

CHAPTER 39

CHAPTER 40

CONCLUSION

Introduction

Mother Teresa was regarded as a modern day saint. This Roman Catholic nun and missionary founded the religious congregation the Missionaries of Charity, which is still in place today despite her death in 1997. The congregation carries on Mother Teresa's good work caring for people with tuberculosis, leprosy and HIV, running soup kitchens, schools and orphanages, giving "wholehearted free service" to those people who are "the poorest of the poor".

Mother Teresa received a number of honors during her lifetime including the Nobel Peace Prize in 1979 and beatification as "Blessed Teresa of Calcutta". While she was a controversial figure due to her stance against contraception, Mother Teresa was greatly admired for her charitable works and became a figure of inspiration around the world.

Although Mother Teresa was born in 1910, her caring and kind wisdom still applies to the modern world. Her teachings can help people to learn to improve their lives, help others and attain true joy.

In this book, you will find forty of Mother Teresa's Inspirational life lessons from her timeless wisdom. Mother Teresa saw the poverty and suffering around her in Calcutta and took action to help one person at a time, inspiring massive change. Regardless of whether you are experiencing a personal crisis or simply wish to enjoy a more fulfilling life, these insightful and inspirational lessons can help you to find joy and fulfillment.

Chapter 1 - Smiling Helps Love to Grow

Mother Teresa believed that love was central to life. She firmly believed that love could be nurtured in all of us. Mother Teresa insisted that we can all help love to grow with even small actions. She said, "every time you smile at someone" it was "a gift" and an "action of love", which made a "beautiful thing". She encouraged us all to smile "let's always meet each other with a smile" as she believed that a "smile is the beginning of love".

Mother Teresa believed that love was of central importance to all life and happiness. She believed that love only needs a little encouragement to fuel great positive changes throughout the world. This is something all of us can do with simple actions such as smiling. You can see this in everyday life. Smiling is contagious. If you are walking down the street and you smile at a stranger, that smile is almost like a Mexican wave as it travels from person to person. Mother Teresa wanted us to smile at everyone, even when it feels difficult to smile. From your family and children, work colleagues through to anyone you meet, smiling is important. She said "it doesn't matter" who that person is, as smiling will help to grow "greater love for each other".

Chapter 2 - Make Time for Your Family

Mother Teresa believed that the family is of the greatest importance. Yet, she appreciated that in this modern busy world, many of us are so engrossed in work, chores and other activities that we sometimes forget to show our families how much they mean to us. She encouraged that even if we are feeling overwhelmed we should try to "make one point" and "make time for each other in your family".

While this can be difficult in those times when you and your spouse are busy, the kids are feeling grumpy and you have to cope with the challenges of work, Mother Teresa felt that this was of great importance. She said that "if we have no peace" it is due to the fact that "we have forgotten we belong to each other".

Although money is important to keep the bills paid, your loved ones are likely to feel that your time is far more precious than any amount of money. As any parent will know, children grow up so fast and one of the biggest regrets people have at the end of their lives is not that they didn't make more money but that they missed out on more time with their loved ones.

Chapter 3 - Actions Speak Louder Than Words

We have all been guilty of big talk sometimes. How many times have we said how terrible some injustice or catastrophe was? While we may talk about these terrible things, how many of us take action?

Mother Teresa inspired others because she saw the poverty and tragedy in Calcutta and didn't just speak about it. It was in taking action that she was able to make a massive difference in the lives of the children living in poverty. Mother Teresa believed that it was possible to "spread the love of God" throughout your life and "only use words when necessary". She firmly believed that the way to demonstrate your love and faith in God was to show kindness and compassion to other people.

This can be applied throughout our lives even in these modern times. While talking about important issues can raise awareness, it is only by taking action that we can truly affect change. Imagine the difference you could make to a homeless person by giving them a meal rather than simply discussing how sad it is with your family or friends. Although words can help for fundraising, it is only by taking action that we can make a real difference.

Chapter 4 - World Peace Starts Small

In these trying times of conflict appearing to simmer under the surface of many nations, the prospect of world peace can be a little overwhelming. However, Mother Teresa believed that massive change and world peace could be accomplished with small actions. She encouraged us to "go out into the world today" and show "love to the people you meet". She believed that it is possible to "let your presence light new light" within the hearts of other people. Mother Teresa believed that "peace begins with a smile" and that showing love to our fellow man could make a massive difference. When asked about the subject of world peace, she said to "promote world peace, go home and love your family". She said that even this small action could have a massive impact on your relationships and the promotion of peace.

While the prospect of trying to achieve world peace is obviously overwhelming, if we all took small actions such as smiling and showing love, the effects would be cumulative and could truly change the world.

Chapter 5 - Love Knows No Boundaries

Many of us view love as an insular concept. While we may love our spouse, children and close friends, it is not often seen as something that can be given to strangers. However, Mother Teresa believed that there were no boundaries to love. She believed that the capacity for love simply grows as we call upon it.

A great example of this is when you have children. When you have one child your love feels full to capacity. Yet when you have another child, the love for the first child does not diminish, you simply have more love to give. Mother Teresa believed that it was possible to give more and more love to make massive change. She said that she had discovered a paradox about love "if you love until it hurts" then you will find that there is "no more hurt, only more love".

This means that while you may feel that your love is complete with your family and close friends, if you begin to show love to more and more people, your capacity will grow. Mother Teresa believed that when you love until you simply cannot love anymore, you will find no pain, only more and more love.

Chapter 6 - Embrace Real Love

In these modern times, it is easy to think that love is abundant and all around us. How many times have you heard someone say, or said yourself, that you love your new gadget, your new car or some other inanimate object? This consumerism is rapidly growing and with the development of social media, love has become a hollow sentiment. However, Mother Teresa believed in the importance of embracing and giving real love. She said that for love to be real, "it must cost" and "it must hurt". True and real love "must empty us of self". It is only by embracing this real love can you truly experience happiness and peace.

While many of us think that we are surrounded by love, it is important to truly assess our situation. Are we embracing real love or simply admiring and adoring hollow pursuits? Ask yourself do you show more love to your car than your next-door neighbor or work colleague? Real love is not superficial and affects us deeply. We must be prepared to pay this cost and endure any pain to truly embrace real love and the amazing benefits it offers.

Chapter 7 - Working Together Can Lead to Great Things

In this modern world, more and more people are becoming self-sufficient. While independence is a good thing, it is important to recognize that working together can lead to great things. We have all seen individual entrepreneurs who have accomplished massive feats and amazing things. This can seem daunting and many of us are reluctant to even try. However, Mother Teresa believed that cooperation and working together could allow even the most humble person to contribute to truly great things.

Mother Teresa believed that it is only by working together can we experience the best of skills and talents. We each have our own particular talents that we are good at and by working together, great things can be accomplished with my skill for one task, your talent for another. Mother Teresa said that "I can do things you cannot and you can do things I cannot", by working together "we can do great things".

Even though Mother Teresa is heralded as making a huge difference in Calcutta and the world, she said "I alone cannot change the world". However, she acknowledged that she could "cast a stone across the water" creating many ripples. This impact can encourage and inspire others fuelling cooperation and working together. Even this small step could help towards great things.

CHAPTER 8 - LIFE FOR OTHERS

With the pressures of the modern world, many of us are focused on our own successes and journeys. You only need to take a walk in any city to watch people so focused on their own lives that they ignore others, even when they are right in front of them. Mother Teresa was a Catholic nun and adhered to the belief that God wants us to help and support others. Only considering yourself is considered to be hollow and cutting yourself off from the love and support of other people. This reciprocation of love and support is truly the only way to feel joy.

Mother Teresa echoed this sentiment by saying that " a life not lived for others, is not a life". She believed that to live life only for oneself would be a hollow experience and you would never truly experience the fulfillment of life. By living for others, others will also live for you. This reciprocation will allow you to experience great love. Being selfless will offer more rewards than the selfish pursuit of material possessions and hollow goals. You are unlikely to regret not having the latest model of car on your deathbed, but you may regret not having offered others the love, support and caring, they could have offered you.

Chapter 9 - Good Deeds May Be Forgotten But This Should Not Stop You

We live in a reward culture. Even small things are recognized with social media and reality television. This has lead to many people only considering doing something if they will get the recognition they deserve. However, truly good deeds need no recognition. Mother Teresa said that "the good you do today may be forgotten" but you should still "do good anyway".

Many people around the world including famous celebrities have adopted this attitude. After the death of the actor Paul Walker, the good works and charity he spent a great deal of time on was highlighted. As people mourned, stories of his helping others and donating his time and money were shared on social media and the Internet. During his life Paul Walker wanted and received no recognition for these deeds but this did not stop him from helping others.

While not all of us have a fantastically paying job or lots of free time, there are still small kindnesses we can do in our everyday life that will make a real difference in the lives of other people. Although you may not receive attention and recognition, helping others in big or small ways can be their own reward. So, next time you see someone struggling to open a door or pick something up from the floor, remember that even small good deeds count with or without recognition.

Chapter 10 - Even Small Deeds Have Meaning

Following on from lesson nine, it is important to realize that even small deeds have significance and meaning. Mother Teresa believed that "it is not how much we give" that is important but "how much love put into giving". She acknowledged that "not all of us can do great things", which may be discouraging, but that we can all "do small things with great love".

Mother Teresa believed that small deeds are the stepping-stone to greatness. She said we should "be faithful in small things" as in them is our strength. Mother Teresa accomplished great things in her lifetime and this good work continues to this day. However, even Mother Teresa was daunted by the massive prospect of starvation and poverty. She said that "if I look at the mass, I will never act", which is why she focused her efforts on the small deeds. She concentrated on one small task at a time to have meaning and contribute to great change.

Mother Teresa also recognized that sometimes even small deeds seem insignificant and can appear to make no difference. She said that there are times when our small deeds are "nothing more than a drop in the ocean". While this may be discouraging to some, she said, "if the drop was not there, the ocean would be missing something". This means that even if our small deed appears unimportant, it still has significance and meaning.

Chapter 11 - Giving Should Hold the Most Importance in Life

With the materialistic attitude we have in modern society, many people are focused entirely on what they have. This means that they concentrate all of their efforts throughout their lives on making money, achieving qualifications and buying things. While there is nothing wrong with aiming to achieve great things, Mother Teresa believed that these things should not hold the most importance in our lives. She believed that giving is the most important aspect of life.

According to Mother Teresa, at the end of our lives, we will be judged by God for entry into heaven. She said that at this time we will not be judged by how much money we have and if we have done great things. Instead we will be judged by the bible quote from Matthew 25:35-40. The quote says, "I was hungry and you gave me something to eat, I was naked and you clothed me. I was homeless and you took me in."

This giving attitude is considered to be the most important aspect of a full life. If you love others and give freely, you will not only experience love and joy but you will know the real important of life and our interactions with other people.

Chapter 12 - Do Not Wait to Take Action

Procrastination is a common issue throughout the world. Many of us are waiting for the perfect time to take some action to achieve any goal. We seem to wait for all the stars to be in alignment and this circumstance or that to be in place before we can take action. However, Mother Teresa insists that it is important to not wait to take action. She said, "Yesterday is gone. Tomorrow has not yet come. We have only today, let us begin."

Mother Teresa believed that "we must live each day as if it were our last". She said that living this way means, "when God calls us we are ready and prepared to die with a clean heart". It is important to realize that circumstances will never be perfect and therefore, you should not wait to take action. According to Mother Teresa, if you want to affect change you should not "wait for leaders, do it alone, person to person". You could have a massive impact on any situation while waiting for the wheels of bureaucracy to catch up.

This approach can be applied to any aspect of our lives. Although primarily Mother Teresa was referring to helping others, not waiting to take action can be applied to all things. Don't wait to spend time with your children and family; don't wait to take some enjoyment from life. At the end of your life, you are more likely to regret the things you didn't do than the things you did.

Chapter 13 - Avoid Judging Others

In our modern culture of social media and reality television, it has never been easier to judge other people. Our world appears to be open for everyone to see, which means that you can see celebrities when they are on their way for a coffee rather than all dressed up for a film premier. This measure of transparency also applies to ordinary people. Look through any social media platform and you will see someone doing or saying something silly. This means that more and more people are developing a judgmental attitude.

Mother Teresa believed that judging people was wrong. She said that if you are judging people "you have no time to love them". Mother Teresa believed that love is one of the most important parts of life. However, not judging others is also important to recognize that we humans are not perfect. Simply no one is perfect and judging others separates us, fueling disharmony.

Although it may be difficult when you are faced with someone doing or saying something very silly, it is important to try to avoid judging others. This encourages empathy, kindness and goodness. Before you begin to judge someone, remember that they are only human.

Chapter 14 - God Only Gives You What You Can Handle

When you are struggling with day-to-day life, it can sometimes feel like you can't cope with anything else. Sometimes crisis seems to follow crisis and it feels like problems are never ending. However, Mother Teresa believed that God will not give anything you can't handle. She even joked, "I wish he didn't trust me so much".

Whether you are struggling with domestic problems, money issues or any other crisis, Mother Teresa believed that it was important to have faith in God. She believed that God understands what each and every one of us is capable of, never pushing us beyond our capabilities. This can often be seen when we experience a problem but something positive comes from it.

Many people often say that things are sent to try us, but having faith that God will not give you something you cannot handle will allow you to see the positive. For example, while your car breaking down on the way to work can be extremely frustrating, it could provide the opportunity to meet a potential new friend or allow you to recognize that it is now time to consider changing from a job you dislike to something closer to home.

Chapter 15 - Be the Expression of Kindness

Mother Teresa believed that it was important to be the expression of kindness in our words, actions and thoughts. She said we should be the "living expression of God's kindness". She advised that we show "kindness in your face, kindness in your eyes, kindness in your smile". Expressing this level of kindness can be challenging but she said "let no one ever come to you without leaving better and happier". These expressions of kindness can be easy to speak and short but "their echoes are truly endless".

Most people can recollect an occasion when someone has been kind to them for no particular reason. From small acts of kindness such as letting you be served before them when you are in a hurry through to helping you with a flat tire or giving you a kind smile. These occasions are nice to recollect and are likely to have made an impression on you for the rest of the day, week, month or your life. Now, imagine having that effect on the people around you. By being the expression of kindness, you can make the world a nicer, happier place.

Chapter 16 - Try to Inspire Others

Mother Teresa didn't just take action to make positive changes for the poor, sick and lonely in Calcutta, but she inspired others to also help those around them. She said, "I alone cannot change the world". However, she was aware that she could "cast a stone across the waters to create many ripples".

The possibility of inspiring others is a little daunting but Mother Teresa said that we should not worry about falling short of our aims or failing. She said that, "God doesn't require us to succeed" rather "he only requires that you try". This means that if you try everyday to inspire other people to help others, aspire towards great deeds or act in a kind loving manner, it doesn't matter if you don't always succeed. Your intentions are far more important. Mother Teresa even said "I prefer you to make mistakes in kindness than work miracles in unkindness".

Make the effort to try to inspire others every day and you may find that even if you fail almost every day, the one day you succeed, you could inspire greatness. If you keep your thoughts kind and aim to inspire, you are likely to feel happiness and more fulfilled than if you never bothered to try.

Chapter 17 - Embrace a Simple Life

With the complexities of the modern world, it is easy to think that everything is an essential to life. However, we don't need the latest television, computer or cellphone. Is it truly important that we are driving the latest model, top specification vehicle? Mother Teresa believed it is important to embrace a simple life. She said we should "live simply so others may live simply".

Recent research has shown that up to forty percent of the groceries in America end up being thrown in the trash. This is a massive amount of wasted food when there are people in the world starving. This wasteful life is decadent and should be considered when we think of people who are less fortunate. In these trying economic times, starving people are not limited to third world countries. There are people in the United States today, who are wondering where their next meal is coming from. Mother Teresa believed that if we embrace a simple life, there will be plenty for everyone.

Next time you are considering spending a great deal of money on the latest device or loading up your grocery cart with food you are probably not even going to eat, remember that if you live more simply, it is not likely to impact on your happiness but could help someone else.

Chapter 18 - Practice Humility

Mother Teresa believed that one of the most important aspects of living a happy and spiritual life was to practice humility. She believed that if you are humble, you will have an innate sense of yourself, so you can feel true happiness. She said, "if you are humble nothing will touch you, neither praise nor disgrace because you know what you are."

For many of us, knowing where to start on the concept of humility is difficulty. However, Mother Teresa believed it is simple. She said, "We learn humility through accepting humiliations cheerfully". This means that you remove pride and vanity from your encounters and can experience genuine interactions.

Mother Teresa instructed that there are a number of ways that we can practice humility. She said "to speak as little as possible of one's self, to mind one's own business" and "not want to manage other people's affairs". She also said you should "pass over the mistakes of others", "accept contradictions and corrections cheerfully", "accept insult and injuries" and "accept being slighted, forgotten and disliked". She said this would allow you to be "kind and gentle even under provocation", "never to stand on one's dignity" and "choose always the hardest".

Chapter 19 - Embrace Happiness

Many of us are striving to achieve happiness and fulfillment. However, many of us fail to embrace happiness, instead spend our time looking for the next reward. Mother Teresa believed that the key to a happy life was to "be happy in the moment" as "that's enough". She insisted that, "each moment is all we need, not more".

This attitude means that you can embrace the small moments of happiness in our lives rather than constantly seeking out a perfect situation. For example, many people believe that if they win the lottery they will be happy. However, while these people spend their days imagining how they would spend their lottery winnings and what their days would be like, they are missing those moments of happiness, which are going on around them. Although we all have bills to pay, spending time enjoying the company of your spouse or playing with your child are truly priceless.

Mother Teresa believed that embracing these moments of happiness will allow you to see the joy in the world. She said "the person who gives a smile is the best giver" since "God loves a cheerful giver". If you learn to see the glass as half full rather than half empty, you will see the positive around you and are likely to have a positive effect on the people around you.

Chapter 20 - Love is Divine

Mother Teresa believed that love is central to life and is the perfect expression of God. She believed that love is divine and when asked about heaven she felt that love would be one of the most important factors. She said that when the time comes for "God to judge us" we will not be asked "how many good things have you done in your life" but rather "how much love did you put into what you did".

Mother Teresa believed that if we did things with love, it was a reflection of God. She referred to herself as a "little pencil in the hand of a writing God", she also believe that God sends a "love letter to the world".

Once you recognize that love is divine, you can begin to see God all around you in everyday life. This means that you can see God in the simplest of things, such as a stranger doing something nice for you.

Chapter 21 - We All Need Love

Mother Teresa lived in an area filled with poverty, hunger and despair. However, she recognized that although we need food and water to survive, these are not the only essentials in life. She believed that "the hunger for love is much more difficult to remove than the hunger for bread".

While many of us are aware of famines around the world, Mother Teresa believed that simply supplying food would not solve the problem. This is because we all need love and for this reason she said, "it is not how much we give but how much love we put into giving". Most people have sufficient if not access to too much food and clean drinking water, but this does not mean that we are happy. This is because food and drink do not give us love. We can only get love from other people, our family, friends, acquaintances and even strangers.

Fortunately, Mother Teresa believed that it is easy to supply plenty of love for everyone. She said that, "every time you smile, it is an action of love, a gift to that person and a beautiful thing". Once you embrace the concept that every single person on this planet needs love, you can learn to more readily empathize with other people. Next time you are thinking about the latest Hollywood celebrity scandal, you can understand that despite massive box office hits, these actors and actresses are just like us and need love.

Chapter 22 - Realize the Impossible Can be Possible

Many of us fail to take action as these goals seem impossible to attain. This means that we develop an attitude of not even bothering, as we believe things to be impossible. However, Mother Teresa did not ascribe to this. She believed it was important to realize that the impossible can be possible. She believed that we must try and have good intentions to perform good deeds. After all, if we try with good intentions and fail, we have still managed to do something.

Mother Teresa recognized that some tasks are impossible, but often there is a solution. She said that even if we don't have all the skills, knowledge or even motivation, we could still accomplish our goals. She said "We, the unwilling, led by the unknowing are doing the impossible for the ungrateful". This did not discourage her and in fact it inspired her to do even more. She said, "We have done so much for so long, with so little, we are not qualified to do anything with nothing." This shows that even with little chance of success, Mother Teresa was always willing to try. Even after all her accomplishments, she was never afraid to try to do more and more to help others.

Chapter 23 - Poverty is Not Just a Lack of Money

Mother Teresa worked as a nun and missionary in some of the most poverty stricken areas of the world. In Calcutta, she saw great poverty and despair but she recognized that poverty is not simply a lack of money. This sentiment means that even those with money can be poor and those with only a small amount of money can actually be quite rich. She said, "The most terrible poverty is loneliness and the feeling of being unloved".

However, Mother Teresa recognized that this can be more difficult to overcome. She said, "The hunger for love is more difficult to remove than the hunger for bread". She believed that this challenge could be overcome but it is actually underestimated around the world, especially in the first world. She said, "The greatest disease in the West today is not TB or leprosy; it is being unwanted, unloved and uncared for." She believed that although "we can cure physical diseases with medicine, but the only cure for loneliness, despair and hopelessness is love."

Mother Teresa believed that this form of poverty is prevalent all around the world. She said that, "there are many in the world who are dying for a piece of bread but there are many more dying for a little love". She believed that poverty occurs all over the world, even in the richest first world countries. She said "The poverty in the West is a different kind of poverty, it is not only a poverty of loneliness but also of spirituality." She believed that there is "a hunger for love as there is a hunger for God."

CHAPTER 24 - DON'T RACE AHEAD

In our modern culture, everything seems to move at a million miles a minute. Everyone always seems to be on the go, rushing from errand to errand. With the miles long traffic jams and thousands of people bustling on the city streets, it is easy to see how we are all racing through life. However, Mother Teresa felt that it was important to slow down and take time out to appreciate life and God. She understood that it was important to have time for silent reflection for yourself and your relationship with God.

Mother Teresa strongly believed in God, Saints and guardian angels. She believed that we all have our own guardian angels looking out for us. However, she warned that we should take care not to rush ahead in life and cautioned that we should "never travel faster than your guardian angel can fly". Whether you have a strong belief in spirituality or not, the lesson of not racing ahead is still important. By racing ahead, we can often miss vital things in life and fail to take the proper time to contemplate. Many gurus and philosophers recognize the importance of living in the moment and taking the time out just for oneself. It is only by having the time for ourselves that we can properly connect with our goals and our spirituality.

Chapter 25 - Embrace Prayer

In the modern world of cynicism, the power of prayer is often overlooked. As religion is taken out of schools and families are less inclined to visit church, many people fail to understand the concept of praying. However, Mother Teresa believed it was important to embrace prayer. Most people consider prayer to be something only done in stuffy quiet churches and chapels. Mother Teresa believed that prayer is a pure way to connect with God. She said that "prayer is not asking", you are not simply wishing for things. She said in fact, "prayer is putting oneself in the hands of God". It is the opportunity to put yourself "at his disposition and listening to His voice in the depths of our hearts".

Mother Teresa believed that prayer could offer great comfort in times of crisis, strength in times of trial and celebration in times of triumph. She felt it was important to embrace prayer as an integral part of all aspects of your life. This would allow you to build a relationship with God, which can help you through all the trials and tribulations of life. This ability to put yourself in God's hands can be remarkably reassuring and help you to cope.

Chapter 26 - God is Goodness

Mother Teresa firmly believed that God simply is goodness. She believed that God cares deeply for each and every one of us. She said "God made the world for the delight of human beings". She believed that God and his goodness is everywhere. She said that in "his concern for us, his awareness of our needs and just the little things" God demonstrated his goodness. She believed that "the phone call we've waited for, the ride we are offered and the letter in the mail" are all examples of the little ways God demonstrates his goodness. She believed that God "does for us throughout the day".

Mother Teresa believed that it is important for us to "remember and notice His love for us". She said that once you notice everything God does for us, "you just can't resist Him". She went further to say "I believe there's no such thing as luck in life, it's God's love".

Mother Teresa had such faith in God's goodness that when asked about heaven, she said, "I am not sure exactly what heaven will be like" but that it would be based on "How much love did you put into what you did".

Chapter 27 - Recognize Good Intentions

Mother Teresa spoke often about having good intentions in everything we do. She believed that our intentions mattered more than the actual results of our endeavors. She spoke many times about how she would prefer that we accomplish nothing with good intentions rather than miracles with harmful intent. However, she also said that it was important to recognize good intentions in others. Although it is tempting to see only what others do or fail to do, if we recognize when something has been done with good intent, we can properly value it.

Recognizing good intentions in others can be challenging and appreciating the other person's efforts can be frustrating at times. Imagine if you came home to find that your spouse had made you a perfectly planned home cooked meal. While it may not always taste wonderful, it is important to recognize that this was done with love for you and to show you their appreciation. By recognizing this, you can reciprocate the love. Mother Teresa said "Do not think that love in order to be genuine has to be extraordinary." She believed that what we actually need is "to love without getting tired". Mother Teresa said we need to, "be faithful in small things because it is in them that your strength lies". So, next time a family member or friend tries to do something nice for you, remember that it was done with love even if they didn't totally manage to accomplish their aim.

Chapter 28 - Be Kind to Others

Although with a busy schedule and demanding job, it can be challenging to concentrate on being kind to others. There is a tendency to rush through our daily lives without giving consideration to how kindly we treat other people. However, if we fail to be kind to others, we are living only a hollow life. Being kind to others is one of the only ways to truly empathize and understand the people around us.

Mother Teresa believed that one of the most important aspects of life was to be kind to others. She spent her life dedicated to being kind to others, she said, "kind words can be short and easy to speak, but their echoes are truly endless". Mother Teresa believed that kindness to others was an essential part of living a truly contented life. She said that we should "be the living expression of God's kindness". She said we should aim to show "kindness in your face, kindness in your eyes and kindness in your smile". Mother Teresa believed that when our lives end, we will be judged not by how much money we have made but by how we have treated other people.

Chapter 29 - We All Have Strengths and Weaknesses

One of the major problems in our society today is that everyone feels that they should be able to do everything. We live in a culture that encourages children that there is no such thing as failure but this concept does not allow for people to experience that we all have strengths and weaknesses. While it may seem idyllic for everyone to be equal whether it comes to running a race or passing a math test, this diminishes our own special strengths and weaknesses. Mother Teresa believed it was important to acknowledge these differences as it encouraged working together. She said "I can do things you cannot, you can do things I cannot; together we can do great things."

If we fail to recognize that we have both strengths and weaknesses, we may fail to recognize the strengths and weaknesses in others. By acknowledging that we may lack the skills to do something, it allows us the opportunity to seek out someone to collaborate with and accomplish something great. Embracing this concept opens us up to more readily accepting and offering help to others. Since, Mother Teresa believed strongly in working together, this could be the ultimate tribute to her inspiring life's work.

Chapter 30 - Put Others First

As a nun and missionary, Mother Teresa led a totally selfless life. She spent all of her time putting the care and welfare of others before her own needs. Mother Teresa believed that putting others first was an important aspect of living a happy and spiritual life. She said that, "a life not lived for others is not a life".

Mother Teresa did appreciate that in the modern world, people are very busy running around working, completing chores and coping with the demands of daily life. However, she said it was still important put others first, especially your loved ones. She said that, "love begins by taking care of the closest ones - the ones at home". While money, of course, is essential for paying the bills and keeping your family fed with a roof over their heads, care and consideration for your family means more than this. Mother Teresa said we should "never be so busy as not to think of others". This should encourage us to take a moment and evaluate even when we are running around working and doing chores. Once you are confident that your family is first, you may even consider spreading this care and consideration further to people in your community or around the world.

Chapter 31 - Participate in Life

With social media, the Internet and 24-hour television, it has never been easier to isolate oneself. Many people now manage to go day to day without seeing or speaking to anyone apart from the occasional delivery person dropping off their groceries, take away or latest gadget order. While this does seem to make life simpler, Mother Teresa would not have viewed this as living. She believed that we need to participate fully in life. She said that "life is a game, play it". This means that we need to interact with other people and enjoy the company of others.

Although you may have thousands of friends in your social media network, these friendships are hollow and they cannot provide the support, care and comfort of real friendships. If you view life as a game, it doesn't matter if you win or lose, you simply play and enjoy.

While Mother Teresa died before many of the social media platforms were developed, it is almost as if she could see how we were beginning to isolate ourselves from other people. She believed that it is by showing love, caring and understanding to others that we could feel God's love. This means that she would have likely found the concept of only communicating via a computer screen to be a real shame.

Chapter 32 - Listen For Your Own Calling

While Mother Teresa knew her calling at a very early age, she did appreciate that many of us have far less firm beliefs. However, she did insist that each and every one of us has our own calling; we simply need to listen for it. She said that, "there is a light in this world, a healing spirit more powerful than any darkness we may encounter." She said that while "we sometimes lose sight of this force when there is suffering and too much pain, suddenly the spirit will emerge through the lives of ordinary people who hear a call and answer in extraordinary ways".

Mother Teresa always spoke of people doing special things big and small. So, while you may worry that you don't have a massive calling like Mother Teresa had, it is important to realize that your calling may involve smaller tasks which can still have a massive impact. Your own calling may involve helping out the elderly in your neighborhood, supporting family and friends or even brightening up the day of the people you meet. Don't undervalue your calling as it could make a huge difference in the lives of the people all around you.

Chapter 33 - Understand Pain and Suffering

One of the main difficulties many people have with faith is the pain and suffering in the world. When we see images of children starving in third world countries and experience the pain of bereavement, it is difficult to see or understand the will of God. Mother Teresa saw great suffering in her lifetime. She saw the devastation of the 1943 Bengal famine and the poverty in Calcutta on a daily basis.

While this may make many people question their faith, Mother Teresa's resolve was hardened further. She understood that her path was to try to relieve some of this suffering. She believed that suffering and pain are actually a way to experience Jesus. She once said "I think it is very good when people suffer", while this statement is extremely controversial, Mother Teresa said that, "to me that is like the kiss of Jesus". She recognized that pain and suffering are in the world. She said that while "pain and suffering have come into your life" you should "remember pain, sorrow and suffering are but the kiss of Jesus, a sign that you've come so close to Him, He can kiss you".

When people question whether Mother Teresa personally experienced pain and suffering, they should be aware that when Mother Teresa left to take her religious vows, she left behind her family and never saw her mother or sister again. However, Mother Teresa harnessed this pain into a positive experience. She said "I must be willing to give whatever it takes to do good to others" This sacrifice required her to "be willing to give until it hurts". She felt that "otherwise, there is no true love in me and I bring injustice not peace to those around me".

Chapter 34 - See God All Around You

Mother Teresa had a very strong faith in God and believed that the key to happiness and contentment was to see God all around you. This provided her with great comfort to cope with the challenges and obstacles on her difficult path. While many people would have stumbled at the first hurdle on her course of trying to make a difference in the massive suffering and poverty in Calcutta, Mother Teresa felt reassured by the presence of God all around her.

Mother Teresa believed that seeing God all around us is an important aspect of finding contentment in our lives. She said that, "we need to find God". However, she believed that God "cannot be found in noise and restlessness". She encouraged us to take time in contemplation, as "God is the friend of silence". She added that we need only look to the natural world, "see how nature, the trees, flowers and grass grows in silence, see the stars, moon and the sun, how they move in silence. We need silence to be able to touch souls".

Mother Teresa also believed that God was not simply a reassuring force, but was also present in each person she saw. She believed that each person was a reflection of God's need. She said "Hungry for love. He looks at you. Thirsty for kindness, He begs of you. Naked for loyalty, He hopes in you. Homeless for shelter in your heart, He asks of you. Will you be that one to Him".

Chapter 35 - Love is Exponential

Mother Teresa believed that love grows exponentially. She believed that the more love you give, the more love you will have to give. In fact, she said that "intense love does not measure, it just gives". This means that we shouldn't be concerned with worrying about how much love we have to give, we should simply give and it will always grow to meet the demand. Mother Teresa said, "love is a fruit in season at all times and within reach of every hand".

While many people wonder about how it is possible to generate enough love to change the whole world, Mother Teresa believed that this is unimportant. She simply believed that if we merely love, the rest will take care of itself. She said that "Jesus said love one another. He didn't say love the whole world", as the reality is that if we loved one another, we can change the whole world.

In this modern world of technological developments and scientific discoveries, it is easy to overlook the simple power of love. However, Mother Teresa said that, "the greatest science in the world in heaven and on earth is love". This creates a wonderful image that love can truly change the world and as we are all striving for fulfillment and joy, it is the best opportunity to achieve this. In fact, Mother Teresa said, "joy is a net of love in which you can catch souls". Once we embrace the prospect that love will grow exponentially, it is easy to see how we can attain fulfillment and joy.

CHAPTER 36 - UNDERSTAND WHY WE ARE HERE

The concept of why we are here has been fuel for debate for hundreds of years. While scientists and philosophers argue the finer points of this existential argument, Mother Teresa believed that there is a simpler reason. She said that in order to achieve happiness and fulfillment "we must know that we have been created for greater things". She encouraged us not "just to be a number in the world, not just to go for diplomas and degrees, this work and that work". Mother Teresa believed that "we have been created in order to love and to be loved".

Once we understand and accept this as the reason we are here, it becomes easier to embrace life and enjoy the experience. Without the worry about needing to discover the "true" meaning of life, you can simply experience loving and being loved. This adds an amazing quality to life and allows us to connect with not only our close friends and family but also all of the other people we meet around the world.

Chapter 37 - Money Is Not Enough

In our consumer driven culture, it appears that money is the most important thing in the world. This means that when we notice suffering or poverty, our first instinct may be to just donate a few dollars and consider this enough. However, Mother Teresa considered that money is simply not enough. She said, "let us not be satisfied with just giving money". She further explained that "money is not enough, money can be got, but they need your hearts to love them." This means that we should "spread your love everywhere you go".

While money is important to help those starving in a famine, Mother Teresa believed that it is also important to express our love rather than just donating a few dollars. This attitude of charity can also be carried through into our communities and those near us in need. Mother Teresa believed it was important to "smile at each other". She recommended that we "smile at your wife, smile at your husband, smile at your children, smile at each other - it doesn't matter who it is and that will help to grow up in greater love for each other". Although there are very rich people in the world who may be able to donate vast sums of money, the value of the small things should not be overlooked. Mother Teresa said that, "there are many people who can do big things, but there are very few people who will do the small things".

Chapter 38 - Give and You Will Receive

Especially if you are on a limited income, the concept of giving can be hard to contemplate. This lack of funds often stops many people from even thinking of giving to charity. However, charity does not necessarily mean that you need to give money. There are plenty of charitable organizations that are always in need of volunteers and your time. This means that even if you can't spare a few dollars, you could still make a huge difference in someone else's life. This giving need not even be in a formal setting. You may have an elderly neighbor who only sees his or her family a couple of times a month. You could make a huge difference to their quality of life by simply having a coffee and a chat with them once or twice a week. As previously discussed in this book, loneliness is a terrible thing and many older people have very limited contact with other people.

Mother Teresa believed that giving offered its own rewards. She believed that if you give then you shall receive. This concept doesn't mean that if you give a dollar, you will get one or two dollars back. Rather if you give of your time and your love to others, you will find it very rewarding. Mother Teresa said that, "A joyful heart is the normal result of a heart burning with love. She gives most who gives with joy."

Chapter 39 - Look For the Light

With the challenges of the modern world, it can be very easy to feel consumed by darkness and only see the doom and gloom in the world. However, Mother Teresa believed that the world is filled with light and joy. She believed that if we celebrate love, giving and joy, we will not only see the light in the world, but can actually help to increase it. Our actions can have a direct consequence on the world, and it is only by loving and giving will we be able to look for the light.

Mother Teresa believed that all of our actions had consequence. She said that, "Words which do not give the light of Christ increase the darkness." She believed that it was important to "Go out into the world today and love the people you meet. Let your presence light new light in the hearts of people." and that our "Profound joy of the heart is like a magnet that indicates the path of life."

While it can be very easy to get sucked into a view of the world that is all darkness and bad deeds, there are inspiring stories to be found all around the world. You need only pick up your local newspaper and there is likely to be a story of someone helping another or someone doing something special for a good cause. Once you start to look for the light, you will be amazed at the light and goodness all around you.

Chapter 40 - Don't Let the Possibility of Failure Stop You

Many of us procrastinate simply because of the possibility that we may not succeed. However, Mother Teresa believed that we should not let the possibility of failure prevent you from even trying. We should not be scared of failure, as it can be a learning experience. Even if the worst happens and all you have been trying to build falls, Mother Teresa said that we should still try. She said "What you spend years building may be destroyed overnight; build it anyway."

Many of us worry about wasting our time trying something, which could fail, but if you have faith and good intentions, even failures can actually be a success. Mother Teresa said that, "When you have nothing left but God, you have more than enough to start over again." If you have a kind heart and giving soul, even the possibility of failure should not stop you from feeling content even if you don't achieve the results you intended.

For example, imagine if you lived near an area with a large homeless population and wanted to help. You may choose to work in a soup kitchen or try to help out even more directly. If you made sandwiches to distribute and only managed to feed a handful of people, the quality of life for those people would still have been improved, even if you didn't manage to feed the whole area. Once you remove the fear of failure, you may be willing to try even small things, which could have a positive impact all around you.

Conclusion

Mother Teresa lived a long life and inspired generations. Although she died in 1997, her good works and the charitable organizations she established continue to help people to this day. While we may not all have the ability and drive to have this massive an impact on the world, the inspirational life lessons and timeless wisdom of Mother Teresa can be implemented into our everyday lives. Mother Teresa encouraged us to love freely, care for one another and inspire to help others. She valued that even small things could have a massive impact and encouraged us to try regardless of the possibility of failure.

Whether you are looking to improve your own quality of life, need spiritual guidance or strive to help others, these forty life lessons should help to guide you to a more loving caring and contented life. Regardless of your religious persuasion, the life and wisdom of this Roman Catholic nun can be an inspiration for anyone. Through her words, deeds and actions, she has inspired thousands of people to try to make the world a better place. If we can all embrace trying to create even a small percentage of this positive change, poverty, hunger and conflict would soon be things of the past.

Regardless of your reason for considering the life lessons of Mother Teresa, I hope this book has helped to guide you through your own personal situation. This timeless wisdom can be applied to any situation and will hopefully help you to achieve a more fulfilled and contented life.

To hear about Entrepreneur Publishing's new books first (and to be notified when there are free promotions), sign up to their New Release Mailing List.

Finally, if you enjoyed this book, please take the time to share your thoughts and post a review on Amazon. It'd be greatly appreciated!

Thank you and good luck!

Preview Of 'Oprah: 40 Inspirational Life Lessons And Powerful Wisdom From Oprah Winfrey' by Scarlett Johnson

CHAPTER 1 - Your Start in Life Should Not Stop You

Oprah is a firm believer that your start in life should not stop you from achieving your goals or realizing your dreams. Oprah herself had humble beginnings in life. Her teenage unmarried mother took her to live with her maternal grandmother in rural poverty. Although her grandmother took Oprah to the local church frequently and taught her to read before she was three, she would be hit with a stick if she misbehaved or failed to complete her chores. Local children also bullied her as her family was so poor that she would be forced to wear dresses made from potato sacks.

While Oprah suffered physical and sexual abuse during her childhood, acting out in destructive ways, this did not stop her from receiving a four-year scholarship. Although she credited living with her father who taught her strength and self-reliance, Oprah has never allowed her start in life to limit her potential or prevent her from achieving her goals.

CHAPTER 2- Be Prepared to Work Hard

Oprah also strongly believes that in order to achieve your goals, you need to be prepared to work hard. Oprah began working on local radio when she was still in high school and landed a job as a co-anchor when she was only nineteen. Oprah was the first female black news anchor and the youngest anchor at WLAC-TV in Nashville. While this position was very factual and needed a cold calm demeanor, Oprah continued to work hard and give the role one hundred percent effort. Oprah moved to WJZ-TV in Baltimore to co-anchor the evening news in 1976 and waited a further two years before being recruited to co-host People Are Talking, the WJZ local talk show. It was this talk show that allowed Oprah to fully explore her enjoyment of allowing her empathetic style to put guests at ease and provide the forerunner for her own show.

As Theodore Roosevelt said "nothing is worth having unless it means effort, pain and difficulty". This means that before you make any steps towards achieving your goal, you will need to be prepared to work hard.

CHAPTER 3 - Surround Yourself With Positivity

Oprah has had her share of dark times in her life. From her troubled childhood through to amazingly successful woman, Oprah has shown remarkable dedication and effort to perform this dramatic shift. However, Oprah also believes that surrounding yourself with positivity can help to achieve your goals. According to Oprah, she is continually "working on not letting people with dark energy consume any of my minutes on this earth".

Most people are aware of negative people in their lives, who will continually make us question our dreams and what we are looking to achieve. Oprah believes that "how you spend your time defines who you are". This means that if you are spending your time surrounded by dark energy consuming negativity, you are likely to struggle to make positive changes in your life. Negativity can be contagious and it is only by surrounding yourself with positivity can you break free of negative patterns of behavior.

CHAPTER 4 - Tomorrow is Filled With Possibilities

Even during the most challenging of days, it is important to remember that tomorrow is filled with possibilities. Oprah has said that she wants "every day to be a fresh start on expanding what is possible". She appreciates that a desensitized "shut down life" is not what she wants from life and would rather work towards achieving that fresh start.

Oprah sees fresh starts as an important topic, with each day bringing "a chance to start over". Since most people spend their time thinking that they are in too deep or have been traveling in the wrong direction for far too long, Oprah insists that this is not the case and showcases this potential by continually striving for new possibilities. Although she has no financial need to continue working, Oprah is continually taking new opportunities, changing herself for the better. While the mind may make it seem like change is impossible, there is nothing in your past, which limits your potential for changing today. Put your thoughts into action and start the harnessing the possibilities now.

Click here to check out the rest of Oprah: 40 Inspirational Life Lessons And Powerful Wisdom From Oprah Winfrey on Amazon.

Or go to: http://amzn.to/1SwvtCf

MORE BOOKS FOR ENTREPRENEURS

Click here to check out the rest of Entrepreneur Publishing's books on Amazon.

Below you'll find some of my other popular books that are popular on Amazon and Kindle as well. Simply click on the links below to check them out. Alternatively, you can visit my author page on Amazon to see other work done by me.

How Audiobooks Make You Smarter: 7 Little Known Ways Audio Books Can Boost Memory Capacity And Increase Intelligence

How To Write A Book And Publish On Amazon: Make Money With Amazon Kindle, CreateSpace And Audiobooks

Gardening For Entrepreneurs: Gardening Techniques For High Yield, High Profit Crops

Speed Reading For Entrepreneurs: Seven Speed Reading Tactics To Read Faster, Improve Memory And Increase Profits

Content Marketing Strategies: How Delivering Sensational Value Can Help You Build A Digital Media Empire

Kindle Publishing For Entrepreneurs: 9 Steps To Producing Best Selling Amazon Kindle Books And Building Incredible Passive Income

Social Media Marketing: 21 Powerful Marketing Tips To Help Skyrocket Traffic, Establish Authority And Build A Media Platform For Your Business

Video Marketing: How To Produce Viral Films And Leverage Facebook, YouTube, Instagram And Twitter To Build A Massive Audience

Oprah: 40 Inspirational Life Lessons And Powerful Wisdom From Oprah Winfrey

Passive Income Assets: Websites - How To Generate Online Income While You Sleep

Passive Income Assets: Building A Simple Passive Income From Real Estate Investing

If the links do not work, for whatever reason, you can simply search for these titles on the Amazon website to find them.

Printed in Great Britain
by Amazon